Welcome Back
to
Brooklyn

by Brian Merlis & Oscar Israelowitz

Israelowitz Publishing

P.O.Box 290-228 Brooklyn, NY 11229-0004

Tel. (718) 951-7072

Library of Congress Catalog Card Number: 93-078793
International Standard Book Number: 1-878741-14-4

Printed in Brooklyn, New York.

Cover Photo: Loschen Chocolate Shoppe, South Brooklyn, ca. 1915
Back Photo: Brooklyn Borough Hall, ca. 1915

CONTENTS

PREFACE

We all have very special feelings and memories of our home towns. Happy and sad, they are so deeply etched upon our psyches that years only tend to reinforce them. In my life, Brooklyn is that home town - that place of memories.

As a naturally nostalgic (and somewhat escapist) type of person, I chase those memories with a passion. Through many years of reading, researching and collecting, I have become very familiar with Brooklyn's past. I continue to make that quest a driving force in my life.

My interest in local history began in my childhood, at about age six. I attribute it to the innate love for the land which is possessed by every human being and that was nurtured in me at such a tender age.

I believe that my deep immersion into Brooklyn's vast historical heritage has rewarded me with a kind of "collective unconscious." I sometimes experience déja vu when I encounter certain antique photographs and objects. They seem to elicit from me vague memories that predate my own existence.

In my dreams I have wandered through streets and neighborhoods of Brooklyn's yesteryear and have even visited its future - only to awaken and find myself in the present. The purpose of this book is to bring a bit of old Brooklyn to the people of today and to fuel the dream machine that dwells within all of us.

I would like to thank the following people who have supported this endeavor and who also have assisted me in many ways: William Asadorian, Ken Brady, Greg Compolo, Louis Castaldo, David Galinsky, Charles and Nellie Huttunen, Oscar Israelowitz, Joan Kay, Allen Kent, Ira Kluger, Ron Marzlock, I. Stephen Miller, Jack and Rita Merlis, Howard Rose, Ron Schweiger, Charles Shapiro, Joel Streich, Robert and Helene Stonehill, Neil Terens, Joe Trapani, Karen and Arthur Ware III, and Nick Zervos. Without your encouragement this work would not have been possible. I would also like to thank my wife Debbie and my children Heather and Joshua for allowing me to keep running out of the house in order to find many of these items reproduced in this book.

BM

EDWARD E. RUTTER, 1924

Edward E. Rutter was the official photographer for the Borough of Brooklyn. He often risked his safety by setting up his equipment at busy intersections or in underground sewers and tunnels. This book is dedicated to the memory of the many men and women who recorded, collected and preserved Brooklyn's Golden Heritage.

INTRODUCTION

WELCOME BACK TO BROOKLYN recognizes that over one out of seven Americans have roots in Brooklyn.

Through direct personal contact or through the historical experiences of their ancestors, millions of Americans have lived, worked or played in Brooklyn. Even more millions have become familiar with Brooklyn's landmark structures ranging from the Brooklyn Bridge in the northwest to the Soldiers' and Sailors' Monument, a Civil War Memorial Arch at Grand Army Plaza in central Brooklyn and ending with the Parachute Jump Tower in southern Brooklyn.

This book spans the period of time known as the great Industrial Age in American history. Following the Civil War, the northeastern United States became the site of a vast industrial production that fueled the reconstruction of the American Republic and its expansion westward to the Pacific Ocean. Brooklyn, as the fourth largest city in the United States, became during this period one of the largest manufacturing centers not only in the United States, but in the world. Great factories, complex transportation facilities, grand government buildings, elegant mansions and magnificent cultural edifices were built with the enormous concentration of wealth that was developed in Brooklyn.

As London, Paris and Vienna were rebuilding their streets into sweeping boulevards lined with neoclassical architectural institutions filled with the treasures of their world empires, Brooklyn was building a Great Bridge crossing the East River estuary, collecting a world renowned art treasure in the Brooklyn Museum and designing a magnificent park along the battleground where American Revolutionary soldiers fought the British. Eastern and Ocean Parkways were the elegant predecessors of the more utilitarian Shore Parkway, Brooklyn-Queens, Prospect and Gowanus Expressways. Railroad lines were extended to connect the cities of Brooklyn and New York to the suburbs of Brooklyn throughout Kings County. A large resort colony grew out of these southern farmlands - hotels, racetracks, amusement parks and restaurants flourished as they served the recreational needs of the nearby urban centers.

Eventually housing developments began to replace the farms and swamps throughout Kings County.

Kings County, originally patented in 1631 as part of New Netherlands under the Dutch, became part of the New York Colony under the British colonial system in 1664. It was reorganized once again as Kings County in the 1680s under revised British rule. In 1777, it became a county in New York State as the American Revolution raged along the Eastern seaboard in the north. Brooklyn was a sleepy Dutch village overlooking the harbor in the seventeenth and eighteenth centuries. It became incorporated as a city in New York in 1834. It was one of the six original townships of Kings County. As the City of Brooklyn grew, it acquired Williamsburgh and Greenpoint into its urban boundaries. By the end of the nineteenth century, the remaining townships of Bushwick, New Utrecht, New Lots, Flatlands, Flatbush and Gravesend joined the rest of the City of Brooklyn. By 1894, all of the land of Kings County was part of the City of Brooklyn. Then, in June of 1898, Brooklyn was transformed from the fourth largest city of America to the largest borough of the greatest metropolis of the civilized world - the City of Greater New York.

Brooklyn has maintained a spirit of its own as it contributes its fortunes to the city, the state and the national treasuries. The character of Brooklyn lies in the way its residents, its workers, and its visitors have adapted their cultural backgrounds to the resources of the borough. Brooklyn has contributed to many facets of American culture - its language, its cuisine, its industry, its art, its entertainment and its recreation. Brooklyn is linked to over 100 recognized international cultures.

When you are welcomed back to Brooklyn, you are not only returning to a special place, you are returning to a unique lifestyle.

As you turn through these pages, WELCOME BACK TO BROOKLYN!

I. Stephen Miller,
President,
Sheepshead Bay Historical Society, Brooklyn, New York

CLINTON STREET

STREET SCENE, 1921
Bath Avenue and Bay 22nd Street

George Washington landed at Bath Beach during his retreat from the British on Long Island. "Modern" Bath Beach began as a bayside resort that dates from the early 1800s. Bath Avenue was the principal thoroughfare before the West End El was constructed on 86th Street. The West End & Bath Beach Railroad tracks ran down Bath Avenue. Later, the right-of-way was used for trolley transportation. Today, Bath Avenue is still a vital road and many small businesses serve the residents of Bath Beach and Bensonhurst.

BAY RIDGE PARKWAY, 1941

The main roadway of the Gowanus Parkway was constructed over part of the old Third Avenue El. It opened to vehicular traffic on November 1, 1941. View looking north from Owl's Head Park.

SHORE PARKWAY - AERIAL VIEW, 1941

The newly-constructed Belt Parkway section had only two lanes in each direction.

H.C. BOHACK CO. STORE, ca. 1910
1124 Bedford Avenue, corner Gates Avenue

In 1907, Henry C. Bohack owned one store at this location and another in Flatbush, at Flatbush Avenue and Regent Place. The company expanded over the years to become one of Brooklyn's most successful supermarket chains.

CABINET CARD PHOTOGRAPH, 1894 (Opposite)

Henry Holler, a Brooklyn photographer, used this attractive design on the cardboard backing used to mount portrait images.

AUGUST HORNBERGER, TAILOR, ca. 1902
246 Reid Avenue

This shop was located on the west side of Reid Avenue, between Halsey and Hancock Streets.

FOOTBALL TEAM, 1900

A group portrait of the Boys' High School football team. Boys' High
School was located at Putnam and Marcy Avenues.

PROMOTIONAL CARD, ca. 1895

ST. PETER'S EVANGELICAL CHURCH, 1922
1008 Bedford Avenue, between DeKalb and Lafayette Avenues

TRADE CARD, ca. 1885

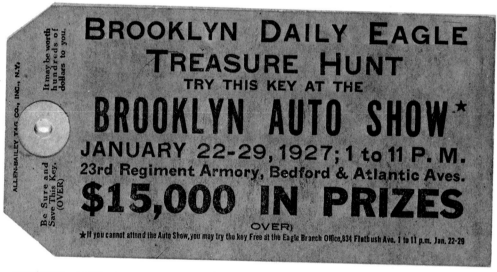

KEY TAG, 1927

BUSINESS CARD, ca. 1900

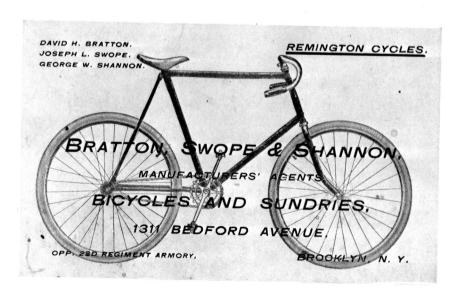

ADVERTISEMENT, 1891

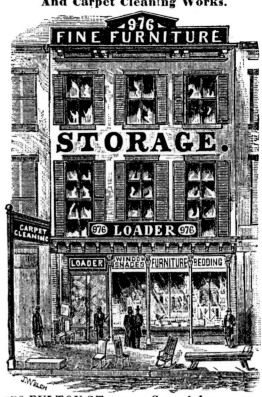

LOADER'S FURNITURE STOREHOUSE
And Carpet Cleaning Works.

976 FULTON ST., near Grand Ave.,
And 399 and 401 McDonough St.

NOSTRAND TROLLEY, ca. 1940s

The Reid/Nostrand Avenue Trolley at the DeKalb Avenue car barn.

LAMBERT TRUBLPRUF TIRE CO. DELIVERY TRUCK, 1919   (Opposite)
1172 Bedford Avenue

LAMBERT TRUBLPRUF TIRE CO. - SHOWROOM, 1919
1172 Bedford Avenue

A major row of automotive showrooms and dealerships opened on
Bedford Avenue as soon as the automobile became popular.

ADVERTISING BLOTTER, ca. 1920s (Opposite)

This advertising blotter is from one of the many car dealerships on
"Automobile Row," along Bedford Avenue.

Maxwell Motor Sales Corporation, 1392 Bedford Ave., Brooklyn, N.Y.

CHARLES W. THORNSTROM'S MEAT STORE, ca. 1915
675 DeKalb Avenue

Many Scandinavian families lived in the Bedford-Stuyvesant section.
This store was located between Nostrand and Marcy Avenues.

STREET SCENE, ca. 1900
1205 Dean Street

ADVERTISEMENT, 1891

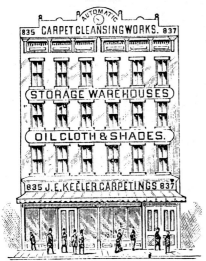
ADVERTISEMENT, 1891

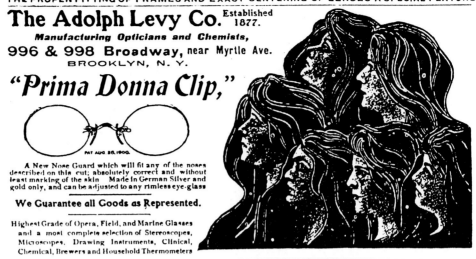
ADVERTISING BLOTTER, ca. 1915

S.R. NEWTON'S BAKERY, ca. 1902
256 Reid Avenue

This bakery was located on the west side of Reid Avenue, between Halsey and Hancock Streets.

ILLUSTRATED BUSINESS ENVELOPE, 1920

W. H. LOTHROP,

Manufacturer of

Plain and Fancy

AWNINGS.

LARGE TENTS TO LET.

Horse, Cart and Truck Covers,

Feed Bags, Etc.

Wall Street Ferry, Brooklyn,

DECORATIONS FOR BALLS, PARTIES, Etc.

Canopies for Weddings and Parties Furnished.

WM. A. BOOTH,

BRASS FOUNDER,

1475 BROADWAY,

Near Gates Ave. L Station.   BROOKLYN, N. Y.

**All kinds of Brass Composition, Bronze
and White Metal Castings furnished
at the Shortest Notice.**

Goods delivered to any part of Brooklyn or New
York City free of charge.

Go to KING S for Everything to Furnish your House.

A. H. KING CO.

Fulton Street and Bedford Avenue,

BROOKLYN.

TRADE CARD, ca. 1885

SHIROTT'S PHARMACY, 1904
Bay Parkway and 86th Street

Shirott's Pharmacy also served as a local U.S. Post Office. It was located on the southeast corner of the intersection.

STREET SCENE, 1927
86th Street and Bay 29th Street

With the construction of the West End Elevated Railroad in 1919, 86th Street soon replaced Bath Avenue as the main shopping street.

TALMUD TORAH SONS OF ISRAEL, ca. 1930s
2115 Benson Avenue

The Spanish tile dome of this grand synagogue was replaced with gold leaf after a tragic fire.

THE BROOKLYN, BATH & WEST END RAILROAD, ca. 1900

54th. Street Station, Borough Park, Brooklyn, N. Y.

10267 Borough Park, 50th Street, Brooklyn, N.Y.

44th STREET STATION, ca. 1910
New Utrecht Avenue and Ft. Hamilton Parkway

Borough Park Club House, Borough Park, Brooklyn, N. Y.

BOROUGH PARK CLUB, 1910
Thirteenth Avenue and 50th Street

In 1898, Senator William H. Reynolds developed the community of Borough Park. He built the Borough Park Club for his new community. That building was later sold to Yeshiva Etz Chaim. One of the alumni of that yeshiva is the noted lawyer, Alan Dershowitz. The building was demolished in the 1970s and replaced with a strip of stores.

TEMPLE BETH EL OF BOROUGH PARK, 1906
Twelfth Avenue and 41st Street

This building was built in 1905 for Temple Beth El of Borough Park. The congregation moved to its lavish building on 15th Avenue and 48th Street in 1920. Some of the noted cantors officiating in Beth El included Moshe Koussevitsky and Moshe Stern.

BATH JUNCTION, 1906
New Utrecht Avenue at 62nd Street

This view of the Brooklyn, Bath & West End Railroad is looking south along
New Utrecht Avenue.

PUBLIC SCHOOL 48, ca. 1930s
Eighteenth Avenue and 60th Street

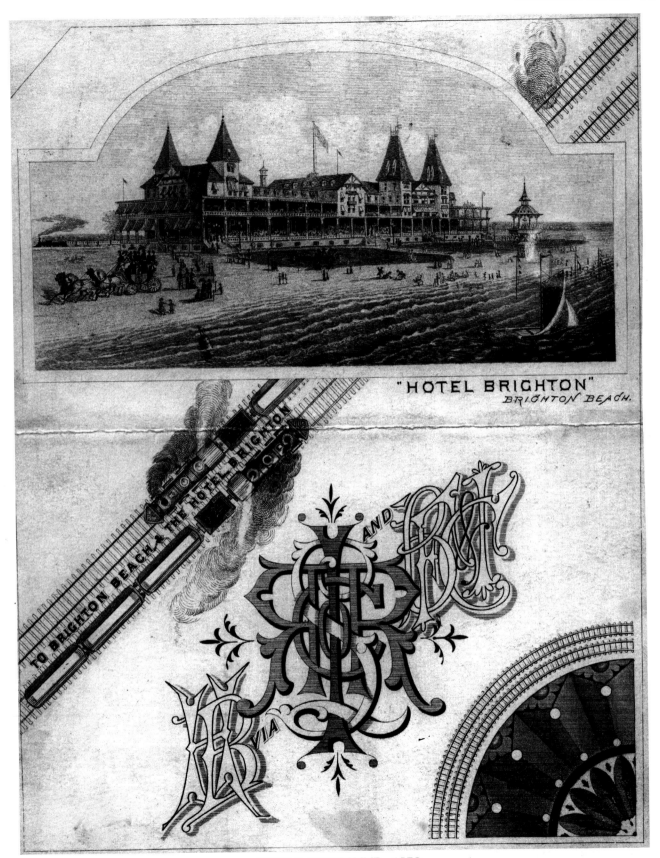

"HOTEL BRIGHTON"
BRIGHTON BEACH.

MENU & PROGRAMME, 1878

A special menu and programme were prepared for the opening of a new railroad route to the Hotel Brighton. This and other improvements in public transportation enabled Brighton, Manhattan and Coney Island beaches to become more accessible to millions of vacationers.

HOTEL BRIGHTON BEACH, 1895

During the 1880s this area was a popular hotel resort. One of these hotels was the Hotel Brighton Beach. During the Great Blizzard of March 13, 1888, the shorefront was totally washed away. The hotel's foundations were exposed and undermined. The hotel was in danger of being swept into the sea. The owner of the hotel decided to save his hotel. He jacked it up, laid railroad tracks under the hotel. He then lowered the hotel on flatbed railroad cars and actually "towed" the entire hotel several hundred feet back to a higher elevation. The Hotel Brighton Beach was demolished in 1923.

MANHATTAN BEACH MARCH, 1893

John Philip Sousa composed the *Manhattan Beach March* in 1893. During the late 19th century, three major hotels were constructed on the eastern half of Coney Island - the Hotel Brighton Beach, the Manhattan Beach Hotel and the Oriental Hotel. None of these hotels is extant.

JAMAICA AVENUE, ca. 1920

Before the construction of the Belt Parkway, the Interborough Parkway and Linden Boulevard, the Jamaica Plank Road was the main thoroughfare which linked eastern to western parts of Brooklyn. It was a toll road for many years. The horses in the photo are headed eastward, towards Queens County.

HOBERMAN'S GREASING STATION, 1928 (Opposite)
East New York Avenue, west of Howard Avenue

The rear of the brick row houses create the illusion of 19th century England, at the peak of its industrial revolution.

DELICATESSEN, ca. 1910
795 Glenmore Avenue

Family-run small businesses were the rule rather than the exception
for many years. Although increased rents caused many to close down,
the "Mom and Pop" store continues to be a part of Brooklyn's cultural
and historical heritage.

HEBREW ORPHAN ASYLUM, ca. 1915
Ralph Avenue and Dean Street

The beginnings of this benevolent society go back to a meeting held on May 16, 1878 in the Keap Street Temple (Beth Elohim). Within one month, two thousand dollars was raised and officers were elected at Stella Hall. In 1889, a committee which included Abraham Abraham (Abraham & Straus) purchased an entire city block in the Brownsville section bounded by Ralph and Howard Avenues and Dean and Pacific Streets for $32,000. The cornerstone was laid on May 3, 1892.

RUSSIAN-AMERICAN PERFORMANCE TROUPE, 1949

This Lower East Side group of singers and dancers consisted of Russian immigrants, most of whom lived in Brooklyn and Manhattan. Rita, the author's mother, is seated on the floor holding a tambourine. Her mother, Hilda Nepo, is slightly right of center and is wearing pearls.

OLD MANSION, 1922

New Jersey Avenue and Fulton Street, northwest corner

This was the former home of Dr. John Andrews. It was built in the early 1870s and originally stood on the east side of Pennsylvania Avenue. It was later moved to the northwest corner of Fulton Street and New Jersey Avenue. A movie billboard was later added onto the structure.

ADVERTISING BLOTTER, ca. 1930

This rare English-Yiddish blotter served the very large Yiddish-speaking population of Brownsville.

CONGREGATION OHAV SHALOM, ca. 1915 (Opposite)
135 Thatford Avenue

At one time, Brownsville was known as the "Jerusalem of America." It had over three hundred congregations within a radius of one square mile. Congregation Ohav Shalom was located just around the corner from Belmont Avenue, crowded with its kosher markets and pushcarts. The building is no longer extant.

THE LOGAN BARBER SHOP, 1938
2601 Pitkin Avenue

The reflections on the building are from the elevated railroad trestle
and railroad signal above Pitkin Avenue.

ASHFORD GARAGE, 1940

View looking north along Ashford Street toward Atlantic Avenue.

MANHATTAN CROSSING, 1915

The Long Island Railroad waiting for the Canarsie Railroad's departure from the Manhattan Crossing.

FORTUNOFF'S, ca. 1950
551 Livonia Avenue

Fortunoff's did not become "The Source" overnight. Many years of hard work by the Fortunoff and Mayrock families paid off and their American dream was finally realized. Quality merchandise at fair prices can be found at Fortunoff's stores throughout the metropolitan area.

TROMMER'S RESTAURANT MENU, 1933

Menu cover from Trommer's Restaurant and Beer Garden. It was
located at 1632 Bushwick Avenue, near Conway Street.

PIEL BROS. BREWERY, ca. 1900
Liberty Avenue, between Georgia and Sheffield Avenues

Brooklyn had dozens of breweries in the pre-Prohibition Era. These companies employed thousands of German-Americans over the years. The Piel Bros. Brewery was located on the south side of Liberty Avenue.

ADVERTISING BLOTTER, ca 1940

OPEN AIR MOTION PICTURE THEATRE, 1913
Saratoga Avenue and Hull Street

"The Movies" were always loved by Brooklynites. Saratoga Amusement Park was located at the northwest corner of Saratoga Avenue and Hull Street, just off Fulton Street.

PHILIP'S DEPARTMENT STORE, 1938
2528 Pitkin Avenue

This store was located at the southwest corner of Atkins Avenue. Note the portable display cases on the sidewalk.

HONIG'S DAIRY, 1938
2530 Pitkin Avenue

"Hot Rolls 1¢ Each" Brooklyn was hard hit during the Great Depression but life went on. Necessities as well as luxury items were still available on Pitkin Avenue, one of Brooklyn's most famous shopping districts.

THE CITY LINE, 1913

In order to escape the teeming crowds of the Lower East Side and Brooklyn's Eastern District, many moved to remote sections of Kings County. Land that had recently been farmland in the old town of New Lots was developed. This photograph shows the new development just west of the Queens border. This neighborhood is still known as "City Line," a reminder that the City of Brooklyn terminated and where Queens County began. The photograph shows the Long Island Railroad on Atlantic Avenue looking east toward Queens at Railroad (Autumn) Avenue.

BROADWAY JUNCTION UNDER CONSTRUCTION, ca. 1918
Broadway and Fulton Street

Following World War I, a major subway and elevated railroad
program was in progress. The Broadway Junction was the site where
the Broadway El, the Lexington Avenue El and the Canarsie El all
intersected. The old open-ended wooden railroad cars were replaced
with much-heavier steel-framed cars. The superstructure supporting
these heavy loads also had to be reinforced with more rigid steel
trestles.

BROOKLYN RAPID TRANSIT RAIL LINES, ca. 1913   (Opposite)

BROADWAY JUNCTION STORAGE YARDS, ca. 1918
Broadway and Fulton Street

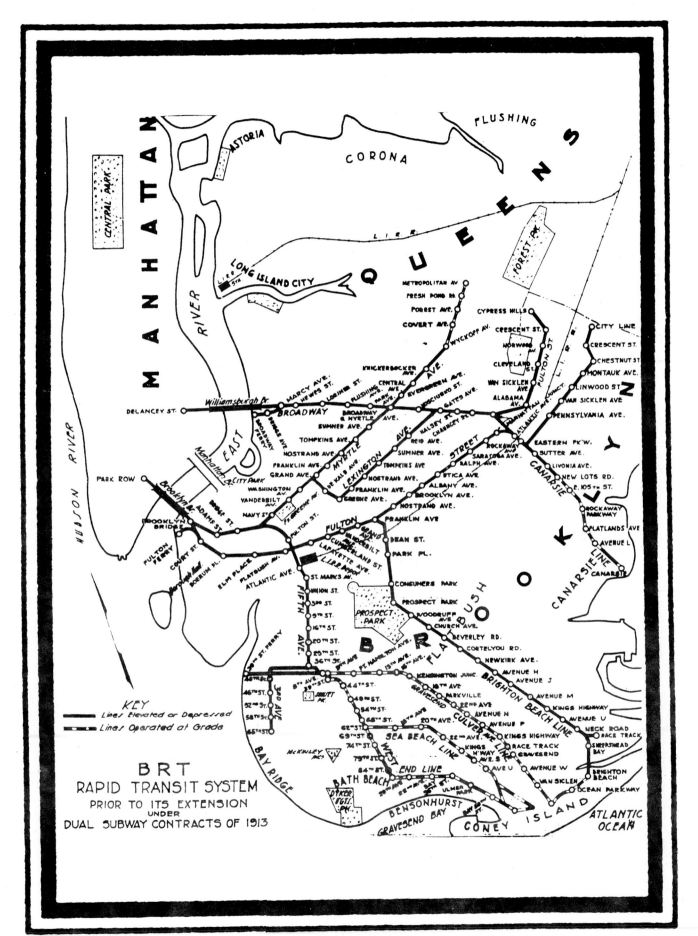

BRT
RAPID TRANSIT SYSTEM
PRIOR TO ITS EXTENSION
UNDER
DUAL SUBWAY CONTRACTS OF 1913

ADVERTISEMENT, 1891

TROLLEY, ca. 1900

Trolley on Ralph Avenue, between Atlantic Avenue and Pacific Street. The Hebrew Orphan Asylum is at right.

THIS WAY TO BUSHWICK AVENUE, 1915

Conway Street, looking north toward Broadway. The Broadway El is
in the distance.

BUSINESS CARD, ca. 1900

VICTORIAN HOUSES, ca. 1890 (Opposite)

These homes were appointed with the most delicate stained-glass windows and woodworking details, inside and out. Note the ornamental wrought-iron front fence.

J. PELIEGER BICYCLES AND MOTORCYCLES, ca. 1910
1604 Bushwick Avenue

As an outgrowth of the bicycle frenzy of the late nineteenth century, the invention of the motorcycle attracted many enthusiastic followers. Here, riders pose just prior to the start of a race to an unknown destination in Nassau County.

WILLARD'S DAIRY WAGON, ca. 1905 (Opposite)

Milk and cream were delivered daily by Otto Gruhn's horse-drawn milk wagon. His office was located at 221-223 Boerum Street, at the corner of the old Bushwick Road.

LIGHT BUOY SERVICE STAND, ca. 1935

The Industrial Home for the Blind trained and employed countless
blind individuals. Many still operate lobby newsstands in office
buildings.
Hanging work gloves indicate that this stand served the many
longshoremen who worked Brooklyn's busy waterfront.

TRAFFIC TOWER, ca. 1928
Bushwick Avenue, looking west toward Jefferson Avenue

Bushwick Avenue was a desirable residential location for many years.
Among its notable residents were New York City Mayor Hylan and Dr.
Cook, who claimed to have reached the North Pole.
Note the unusual traffic control tower in the intersection.

COVERT FARM, 1922
1410 Flushing Avenue

This Dutch homestead was probably the last one in Kings County to be operated as a commercial farm.

BUSHWICK DUTCH REFORMED CHURCH, 1907
Conselyea and Humboldt Streets

The old Bushwick Dutch Reformed Church was erected in 1840 and replaced the original octagonal structure. This view is from Metropolitan Avenue.

STREET SCENE, 1922
Bushwick Avenue and Stagg Street

This view is on the east side of Bushwick Avenue, looking north from Stagg Street. St. Catherine's Hospital is in view at Ten Eyck Street. *Ten Eyck* is Dutch for "At the Oak."

HEADQUARTERS OF "THE CHAT," ca. 1940
Weirfield Street, north of Broadway

The Chat was a Civil Service newspaper similar to *The Chief* of today. The photograph shows the delivery trucks and their drivers ready to begin their rounds.

E. THEODORE BRUNING'S CASH GROCERY, ca. 1908
Conklin Avenue and Rockaway Parkway

Canarsie, located in the eastern part of what was once the Town of Flatlands, retained much of its rural charm even until World War II.
Bruning's Cash Grocery was a general store. When this photo was taken neither the street nor the sidewalk was paved. Note the policeman on the corner.

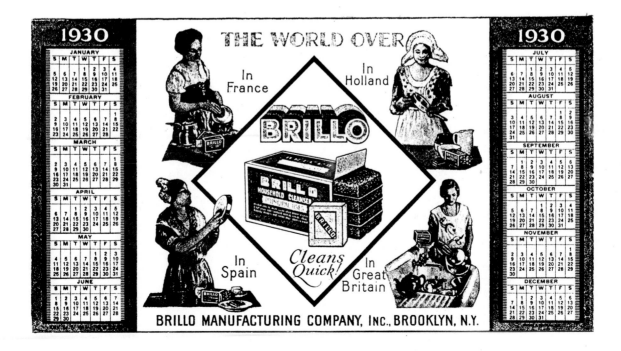

OLD HOUSE, 1922
Rockaway Parkway, south of Skidmore Lane

The area around Rockaway Parkway and Avenue J was once known as the Canarsie Meadows. It was home to many African-American families around the turn of the century.

GANGLER Offers Every Friday Nite

MOONLIGHT RIDING

FREE PLUS
Riding Instructions
Drinks & Eats
Barn Dance

1400 E. 88th STREET
Brooklyn, N. Y.

GANGLER'S DUDE RANCH

Phone
CLoverdale 7-0793

ADVERTISING BLOTTER, ca 1940s

QUONSET HUTS, ca. 1946
Rockaway Parkway

After World War II, temporary housing was provided for veterans and their families. These "Quonset Huts" were built near the Canarsie shore, along Rockaway Parkway. In the spring of 1946, an estimated 413 Quonset Huts were built. Later, the Bayview Houses were constructed on this site.

WILL WARNER'S CARRIAGE, ca. 1920
Rockaway Parkway and Avenue K

STREET SCENE, ca. 1908
Avenue L and East 96th Street, looking west.

The Avenue L Station of the Canarsie Railroad is visible at left. This train terminated near Golden City Park, an amusement park situated at Jamaica Bay. The building at right is still extant and is occupied by a tavern.

WM. M. LITTLE, Auctioneer.

☞ POSITIVE SALE OF AN ☜

Elegant Residence, 8 Lots & Stable

AT AUCTION, ON

CLINTON AVENUE

BROOKLYN,

By order of ELWOOD COOPER, Esq., who intends to leave the city.

Wyckoff & Little

WILL SELL ON

Thursday, March 24th, 1870,

AT TWELVE O'CLOCK. AT THE

Exchange Sales Room, 111 Broadway, N.Y.

One of the most desirable Brooklyn Residences ever offered at Auction, on West side of **CLINTON AVE.**, 200 ft. S. of Greene Avenue, within 30 minutes of Wall Street, and a few blocks from PROSPECT PARK.

☞ See enclosed map and description on opposite cover.

For further particulars apply to the Auctioneers, 151 Montague St., Brooklyn, and 74 Cedar St., New York, where permits to view the premises can be obtained.

LUNA PARK, ca. 1925

This aerial view of Luna Park is looking north along Jones Walk,
toward the park entrance on Surf Avenue.

CIRCUS SIDE SHOW, 1948

The side show offered curious onlookers the chance to see strange
performing acts as well as human oddities. A "barker" is promoting
the Park Circus side show.

CONEY ISLAND - AERIAL VIEW, 1959 (Next Page)

VANDERVEER HOTEL, 1923
Surf Avenue and West 8th Street

The Vanderveer Hotel was built in 1875. It was later called the Sagamore Hotel.

GEORGE C. TILYOU'S STEEPLECHASE PARK, ca. 1955

Opened in 1897, Steeplechase Park outlived the other Coney Island amusement parks, Luna Park and Dreamland. The fourteen acre shrine lasted for over sixty years. It closed in 1965. All that remains is the old Parachute Jump, Brooklyn's version of the Eiffel Tower. The Parachute Jump was originally built for the 1939 World's Fair at Flushing Meadow Park. It was moved to Coney Island after the World's Fair closed.

EBBETS FIELD. ca. 1922
Sullivan Place and Bedford Avenue

This historic baseball stadium was home of the Brooklyn Dodgers. This is the historic landmark Brooklynites wish had never been demolished. This view is of the right field wall.

EBBETS FIELD, ca. 1925
Sullivan Place and Bedford Avenue

This view of Ebbets field was taken from the roof of the Bond Bakery building on Flatbush Avenue.

CORNER CANDY STORE, ca. 1930s
Schenectady and East New York Avenues

Typical six-story apartment house, complete with elevators and a corner candy store downstairs. This building is located on the southeast corner. Maple Street is at the far end of the building.

ADVERTISEMENT BLOTTER, ca. 1925

THE NEW BROOKLYN BRIDGE, 1883

Wittemann's rendering of the new Brooklyn Bridge as it appeared in
1883 from the Fulton Ferry.

BROOKLYN BRIDGE UNDER CONSTRUCTION, ca. 1875

View of the City of Brooklyn from the partially completed Brooklyn
Bridge Tower. Fulton Street is on the right.

CLIPPER SHIPS AT THE COLUMBIA STORES, ca. 1870
Atlantic Street

Grain elevators along the Brooklyn waterfront. Atlantic Street has since been changed to Atlantic Avenue.

FULTON FERRY HOUSE, ca 1875

View of the Fulton Ferry House with the Brooklyn Bridge under construction on right.

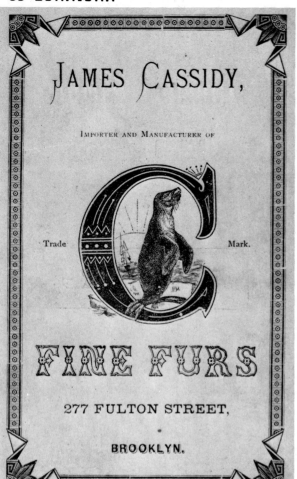

JAMES CASSIDY,

IMPORTER AND MANUFACTURER OF

Trade   Mark.

FINE FURS

277 FULTON STREET,

BROOKLYN.

TRADE CARD, 1880

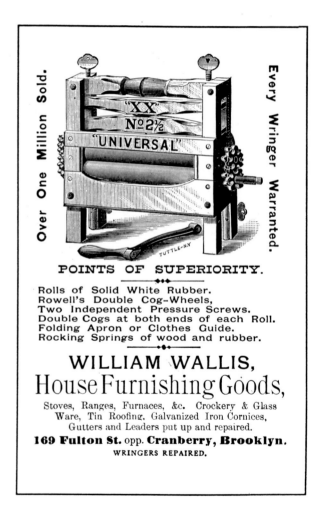

Over One Million Sold.

Every Wringer Warranted.

XX
No 2½
'UNIVERSAL'

TUTTLE-NY

POINTS OF SUPERIORITY.

Rolls of Solid White Rubber.
Rowell's Double Cog-Wheels,
Two Independent Pressure Screws.
Double Cogs at both ends of each Roll.
Folding Apron or Clothes Guide.
Rocking Springs of wood and rubber.

WILLIAM WALLIS,

House Furnishing Goods,

Stoves, Ranges, Furnaces, &c.   Crockery & Glass
Ware, Tin Roofing, Galvanized Iron Cornices,
Gutters and Leaders put up and repaired.

169 Fulton St. opp. **Cranberry, Brooklyn.**

WRINGERS REPAIRED.

ADVERTISEMENT, 1891

BESSIE DARLING.

KESNER'S

Popular Shoe Store,

11 & 13 MYRTLE AVE.,

[OVER]   Near City Hall.

TRADE CARD, ca. 1880

RAINY DAY IN DOWNTOWN BROOKLYN, ca. 1915
Fulton and Adams Streets

For Good Service - - - Phone 3813 Prospect

214 Greene Avenue
240 Sumner Avenue

Brooklyn, N. Y.

ADVERTISING BLOTTER, ca. 1920

ADVERTISEMENT, 1891

Oscar Comstock,
Fish and Oyster Dealer.

354 Fulton St., cor. Red Hook Lane,

Telephone 762.   **BROOKLYN.**

Long Island Eggs Fresh Every Morning.

Blue Point Oysters on the Half-
Shell a Specialty.

**All kinds of Fish and Oysters in their
Season, fresh from the water daily.**

Messengers will call and deliver Orders.

Particular attention given to orders by Mail.

ADVERTISEMENT, 1891

Telephone No. 269 Brooklyn.

F. J. KING,
Furnishing Undertaker,
AND
EMBALMER.

**INTERMENTS PROCURED IN ALL
CEMETERIES.**

Bodies Prepared for Cremation.

Coaches to Let at all Hours, Camp Chairs on Hire.

279 Court Street,

Bet. Butler and Douglass Sts.   BROOKLYN.

BROOKLYN CITY HALL, 1883

Wittemann's rendering of Brooklyn's City Hall. It became Borough
Hall in 1898, when Brooklyn became part of New York City. The old
Court House appears to the left of City Hall.

WASHINGTON BUILDING, 1922
Court and Joralemon Streets

The Washington Building was built in 1851 and was demolished in
1924 to make way for the present Municipal Building. The tall
building is Brooklyn Polytechnic.
View is on east side of Court Street, looking south from Joralemon
Street toward Livingston Street.

BROOKLYN RAPID TRANSIT TERMINUS, 1922
High and Washington Streets

This photograph was taken from the roof of 168-172 Adams Street.
The old house at 161 Washington Street was the home of U.S. Senator
of Rhode Island, Peabody Wetmore.
The train leaving the Bridge Terminal is heading east along High
Street.

M. HIRSCH,
MANUFACTURER OF
CIGARS,
QUEEN'S CUP & ANNEX
ALL TOBACCO
CIGARETTES,
9 FULTON ST.,   BROOKLYN.

ADVERTISEMENT, 1891

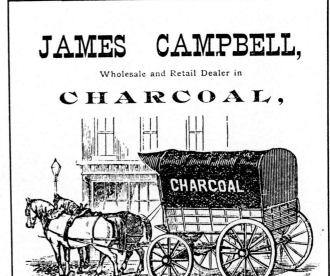

JAMES CAMPBELL,
Wholesale and Retail Dealer in
CHARCOAL,

DEPOT,
43 & 45 BRIDGE ST., BROOKLYN.
ALSO
45 Essex St., Jersey City, New Jersey.
Estimates given and Coal shipped to all parts.
A large variety of Large Coal, Fine Coal and Dust.
COAL BY THE LOAD, BARREL
CRATE OR CARGO.

ADVERTISEMENT, 1891

STOCK CERTIFICATE, ca. 1895
The Nassau Electric Railroad Company owned and operated
numerous trolley lines in Kings County.

CANDY STORE, 1922 (Opposite)
74 Middagh Street

This building originally housed Old No. 3 Engine House. As
firefighting apparatus became larger the building became obsolete. It
was converted into a store and residence early in this century.

TRADE CARD, ca. 1885
Wechsler & Abraham became Abraham & Straus.

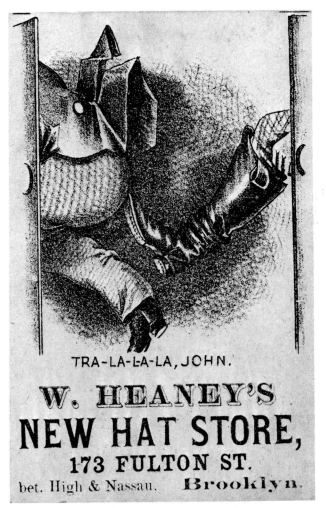

TRA-LA-LA-LA, JOHN.

W. HEANEY'S
NEW HAT STORE,
173 FULTON ST.
bet. High & Nassau. Brooklyn.

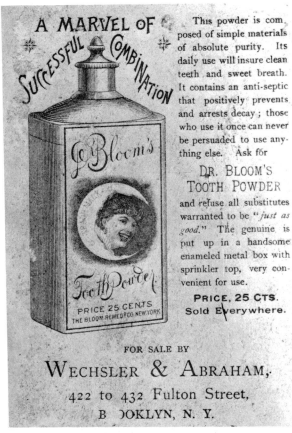

A MARVEL OF
SUCCESSFUL COMBINATION

Dr Bloom's
Tooth Powder

PRICE 25 CENTS
THE BLOOM REMEDY CO. NEW YORK

This powder is com-
posed of simple materials
of absolute purity. Its
daily use will insure clean
teeth and sweet breath.
It contains an anti-septic
that positively prevents
and arrests decay; those
who use it once can never
be persuaded to use any-
thing else. Ask for

Dr. Bloom's
Tooth Powder

and refuse all substitutes
warranted to be "*just as
good.*" The genuine is
put up in a handsome
enameled metal box with
sprinkler top, very con-
venient for use.

PRICE, 25 CTS.
Sold Everywhere.

FOR SALE BY
WECHSLER & ABRAHAM,
422 to 432 Fulton Street,
BROOKLYN, N.Y.

TRADE CARD, ca. 1880

BUSINESS CARD, ca. 1890

Ovington Brothers
Wedding Reception
and Visiting Cards
Arms, Crests,
Monograms
&c.
Stationery
Department
NEW YORK,
BAR HARBOR,
NARRAGANSETT PIER.
Flatbush & Fulton Ave.
Brooklyn

GROCERY, 1940 (Opposite)
299 Hudson Avenue

Interior of the Italian-American Grocery.

BRIDGE CIGAR STORE, 1922
145 Washington Street

The Samuel Bowne House was built around 1840. It was located at 145 Washington Street, at the southeast corner of Sands Street. This house stood directly opposite the entrance to the Brooklyn Bridge.

A.I. NAMM & SONS DEPARTMENT STORE, 1916
Northeast corner Hoyt and Livingston Streets

Namm's, Loeser's, Cowperthwait's, Batterman's, Balch-Price and Browning-King are just a handful of great department stores that once served Brooklynites.

ADVERTISEMENT, 1891

R. H. HAND,

THE OLDEST

Trunk Manufacturer

IN BROOKLYN,

For Strength
and
Durability,

Challenges
all
Competitors,

A GENERAL ASSORTMENT OF

Trunks and Bags of the Best Quality

At moderate prices.   Also a cheaper class of
Goods of all kinds.

Trunks Made to Order at Short Notice.

Also Trunk Covers. Trunks repaired or taken in exchange.

STEAMER CHAIRS AND TRUNKS.

Postal Card will receive immediate attention.

R. H. HAND,

184 FULTON ST.,   BROOKLYN.

CORNER ORANGE STREET.

TRADE CARD, ca. 1880

TRADE CARD, ca. 1880

FIRE HEAD-QUARTERS, 1920 (Opposite)
365 Jay Street

Fire Department Brass at the ornate Romanesque Revival entrance to the Fire Department Headquarters. It was designed by Frank Freeman in 1892. This building is a designated New York City Landmark.

VOLUNTEER FIREMAN, ca. 1890

SEARCHLIGHT #2, 1930 (Opposite)
365 Jay Street

CORNER GENERAL STORE, 1920
Front and Main Streets (southwest corner)

These old buildings were constructed when Brooklyn was still a
village, before 1835.

BLOCK PARTY, ca. 1918
State Street, looking west from Third Avenue

ADVERTISEMENT, ca. 1870

CHAS. W. HELD,

Publisher and Dealer in

SHEET MUSIC,

Music Books, Musical Merchandise, Etc.

Sole Agent for the Unrivalled

KRANICH & BACH and **PEEK & SON,** OPERA PIANOS.

———AND———

MASON & HAMLIN, Organs.

Cash or Time.   Orders by Telephone.

227 FULTON STREET,

BROOKLYN.

ADVERTISEMENT, 1891

P. J SULLIVAN & BRO,

Manufacturers of

FINE CIGARS,

And Dealers in

Leaf Tobacco,

TRADE   MARK.

56 FULTON STREET,

BROOKLYN.

Telephone Call, 1145 Brooklyn.

SPECIALTIES:

Shaughraun, Particular and Modelo Perfecto.

FINE HAND MADE CIGARS A SPECIALTY.

ADVERTISEMENT, 1891

Interior view of Huyler's *863 Broadway, N.Y.*

Branches
150 BROADWAY, N.Y.
ROCHESTER, N.Y.
ALBANY, N.Y.
TROY, N.Y.
BUFFALO, N.Y.
SARATOGA, N.Y.
LONG BRANCH, N.J.

Branches
339-341 FULTON ST.
AND
456 FULTON ST.
BROOKLYN. N.Y.
BOSTON. MASS.
PHILADELPHIA. PA.
WASHINGTON. D.C.
NEWPORT. R.I.

NOVELTIES IN
Bonbons & Chocolates
Fancy Baskets & Bonboniers
FOR PRESENTS

MAKERS OF
Cocoa & Chocolates.
From the Bean
PURE HEALTHFUL.

CELLULOID TRADE CARD, ca. 1885

ADVERTISEMENT, 1891

TRADE CARD, ca. 1885

SAM'L A. BYERS,
FINE SHOES,
527 FULTON STREET,
NEAR DUFFIELD, BROOKLYN

ESTABLISHED 1873.
G. ALFRED SMITH,
Plumbing, Steam and Gas Fitting,
No. 99 Pineapple Street,
Near Fulton Street, BROOKLYN, N. Y.

SANITARY WORK A SPECIALTY.
Remodeling of Country Residences with Plumbing and Steam.
I give Personal Attention to all Work and guarantee satisfaction to my patrons.
All kinds of Jobbing Executed with Dispatch.
BEST OF REFERENCE GIVEN.

SHOPPING ON FULTON STREET, 1925

These stores were located opposite Borough Hall Park. The store at the far right (#357 - French Shriners Shoes) is the north end of the Arbuckle Building, which was once Dieter's Hotel.

By the 1920s, the ornate signs of a previous era were beginning to disappear. When the Fulton El came down in 1941, the entire character of the district changed and by 1955, these buildings were removed for the Civic Center improvement.

All claims for errors should be made within ten days after receipt of Goods.
To receive prompt attention, all communications should be addressed to the firm.

Brooklyn, New York City, Nov. 30, 1898 *189__*

ABRAHAM AND STRAUS·

Sold to

M̲ W. H. White

N̲o̲ 70 7th Avenue

BILLHEAD, 1890s

A & S DELIVERY WAGON, ca. 1900

Founded in 1865, Abraham and Straus is the last of the old-time Downtown department stores. For many years, goods were delivered to all parts of the city by horse-drawn wagon.

LONG ISLAND RAILROAD TERMINAL, 1942

The pink-face brick and terra cotta tile gleam following sandblasting.
The building was recently demolished.

STORES ALONG FLATBUSH AVENUE, 1957

This view of the east side of Flatbush Avenue, looking south from
Fulton Street, shows the familiar merchants; Buddy Lee, J. Michael's
and Hodor. They were located just a few steps from the IRT subway
kiosks.

ROW HOUSES, 1922
136 Clinton Street

These exquisite row houses were built around 1845 opposite St. Ann's Church. At left is St. Charles Borromeo Roman Catholic Church, on Livingston Street.

J.W. REID FURNITURE, 1922
Willoughby and Pearl Streets (northeast corner)

The Central Presbyterian Church was built in 1838 by Samuel A. Willoughby. It was known as the Fifth Presbyterian Church and was demolished around 1928.

COURT STREET TROLLEY, ca. 1950s

Probably the cleanest and most efficient means of transportation ever used in Brooklyn, the electric streetcar was last used on the Church Avenue Line in 1956.
The Post Office and the Brooklyn Daily Eagle Building are in the distance.

FULTON STREET ELEVATED, 1894
Fulton Street, Flatbush Avenue and Nevins Street

B.M. Cowperthwait's Department Store was founded in 1807 and specialized in dry goods, home appliances and furniture. This view is looking west from Fulton Street.

ELEVATED OVERPASS, 1894
Fulton Street and Flatbush Avenue.

The lower trestle was the old Fifth Avenue Elevated Railroad. Above was the Fulton Avenue El. In the background is the north side of Fulton Street, between Hudson Avenue and Rockwell Place. B.G. Latimer & Sons Furniture Store is on the far right.

TALMAGE CHURCH, 1922
327-333 Schermerhorn Street

Reverend T. DeWitt Talmage's Presbyterian Tabernacle was located at this site. It was later used by the Department of Public Charities.

POLICE HEADQUARTERS, 1944
76 Court Street (at Livingston)

This building was built as the Central Grammar High School, a genesis of Boys' High and Girls' High Schools. It later was the cradle of Manual Training High School. It also housed the Police Headquarters of the City of Brooklyn.

HANDBILL, 1870s

- Remember the Notice and Come One! Come All!! -

A PATRIOTIC SOCIAL,

will be held

At St. Mark's Chapel, Adelphi St., near DeKalb Ave.

Wednesday Evening, Feb. 22, 1905.

Door opens at 7:30 o'Clock.

George Washington

ADMISSION 25 CENTS, - PAYABLE AT THE DOOR.

UNDER THE AUSPICES OF THE

BROOKLYN GUILD OF DEAF-MUTES.

BROOKLYN TECHNICAL HIGH SCHOOL, 1933
29 Fort Greene Place

This $5 million high school was opened in 1933, during the
heart of the Depression. Its first principal was Dr. Albert L.
Colston. The bottom photograph epitomizes New York City's
play area problem. Children needed more open spaces and
recreational facilities. The roof of the Brooklyn Technical
High School was used as the play area.

THE ALBEE THEATRE, ca. 1922
Albee Square (DeKalb Avenue and Fulton Street)

The Albee Theatre was located near the old Paramount Theatre. The Paramount is now part of the Long Island University complex.

MYRTLE AVENUE EL, ca. 1900

This view of the old Myrtle Avenue El is looking east from the Bridge Street station. The El was dismantled in the 1970s.

Fifth Avenue Theatre

Next Week Beginning Monday Matinee, June 2nd

MATINEES DAILY EXCEPT FRIDAY

The Popular Fifth Avenue Stock Company

WILL PRESENT

THE GIRL IN THE TAXI

It's Spicy   It's Racy

Trifle Suggestive   Quite Snappy

But Always Within the Bounds of Propriety

EXTRA!   **EXTRA!**   **EXTRA**

Miss Gertrude Morgan and her *Cabaret*
Specialty in the *Lively Cafe Scene.*

SEE IT BY ALL MEANS—It's pleasing to the eye as well as the ear.

Wm. S. Powell,   Henry Titus.

POWELL & TITUS,

DEALERS IN

COAL and WOOD,

Family Trade a Specialty,

YARD, POCKETS and WHARF,

THIRD AVENUE and SECOND STREET.

Gowanus Canal,

Office, 706 Fulton Street,

Near Oxford,   BROOKLYN.

Yard Telephone, 630 Brooklyn.

Office Telephone, 550 Brooklyn.

ADVERTISEMENT, 1891

C. * H. * RIVERS'

ACADEMY FOR DANCING,

175 State cor. of Court Street,

ONE BLOCK FROM ATLANTIC.

Branch School, Ninth St., cor. 7th Ave.

Instruction Imparted Privately or in Classes.

CIRCULARS MAILED.

Inclose twenty-five cents for a revised edition of the

MODERN DANCES.

ADVERTISEMENT, 1891

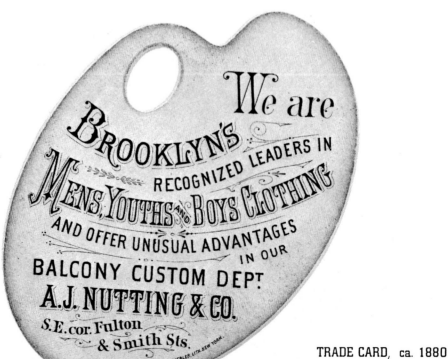

We are BROOKLYN'S RECOGNIZED LEADERS IN Mens, Youths and Boys Clothing AND OFFER UNUSUAL ADVANTAGES IN OUR BALCONY CUSTOM DEPT A.J. NUTTING & CO. S.E. cor. Fulton & Smith Sts.

TRADE CARD, ca. 1880

BROOKLYN QUEENS EXPRESSWAY, 1959
Cadman Plaza

In 1959, the Brooklyn-Queens Expressway was still under construction. The entrance ramp to the Brooklyn Bridge (northbound-at lower left) was not yet completed. The elevated section of the BQE (upper right), along Park Avenue, shows the vertical steel columns still being erected. The Brooklyn Navy Yard is in the upper left corner.

SCHECHTER BROS. POULTRY COMPANY, 1935
858 East 52nd Street

In a landmark Depression Era U.S. Supreme Court case, the four Schechter Bros. were able to put an end to the National Recovery Act. Their Rugby Live Poultry Co. was located south of Foster Avenue. The Schechters also operated a retail store at 257 Brighton Beach Avenue. The case was still in litigation when this photograph was taken.

SCHENCK HOUSE, 1925
Church Avenue, looking east from Utica Avenue

The John Schenck House was located on the northwest corner of East 53rd Street. East Flatbush was named "Rugby" by its promoters at the turn of the century.

SALOON AND SUMMERGARDEN, ca. 1900

This building was demolished and replaced with the entrance to the Botanic Gardens. View is from the corner of Flatbush and Ocean Avenues.

ALBEMARLE THEATRE, 1942
Flatbush Avenue and Albemarle Road

Flatbush Avenue once hosted a number of cinemas. The Albemarle Theatre was a popular rendezvous for Brooklynites during the Golden Age of Movies.

CHURCH AVENUE TROLLEY, 1956
Church Avenue near Flatbush Avenue

On its last year of operation, the trolley is about to pass Garfield's Cafeteria and the old Dutch Reformed Church.

WORLD WAR II BLACKOUT, 1942
Flatbush and Church Avenue

This is how Flatbush Avenue looked at 9:20 pm, after the lights came back on after a wartime blackout test. View is looking south on Flatbush Avenue towards Church Avenue.

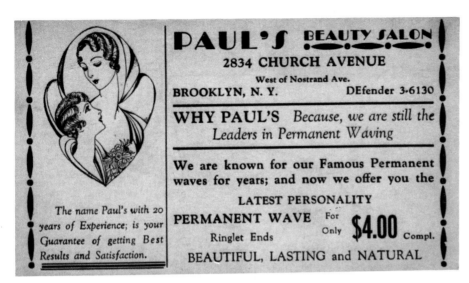

ADVERTISING BLOTTER, ca. 1940

WILBUR HOUSE DEMOLITION, 1923
684 Flatbush Avenue

One of Brooklyn's magnificent Victorian mansions, the Lionel Wilbur
House, was demolished on April 10th 1923.

ADVERTISING BLOTTER, ca. 1930

MEDER'S ICE CREAM PARLOR, 1907
1462-4 Flatbush Avenue

The building is adorned with flags in preparation for the *Flatbush Carnival.*

STREET SCENE, 1923
East side of Flatbush Avenue, opposite Avenue P

THE JUNCTION, 1895
Flatbush and Nostrand Avenues

This is the earliest known photograph of "The Junction." The street at left was then known as Woodbine Place but was soon changed to Germania Place, after Henry Meyer's Company name. In 1957, it was renamed Hillel Place.

The original Flatbush and Flatlands Turnpike road existed since the area was occupied by the Canarsie Indians. In the 1870s, the road was widened and straightened to become today's Flatbush Avenue. Gradually, the old turnpike was discontinued. The only remaining vestige of it is Amersfort Place, which runs for a short distance near Brooklyn College.

BARREN ISLAND, 1931
Main Street

Barren Island was once inhabited by a large number of Irish immigrants. The Catholic church served this Jamaica Bay community.

RYDER HOUSE, ca. 1923
Avenue M and East 29th Street

The J. Ryder House was built in 1860. It was located partially in the roadbed of East 29th Street, 280 feet north of Avenue M. It was demolished in order to make room for new housing development.

TRADE CARD, ca. 1900

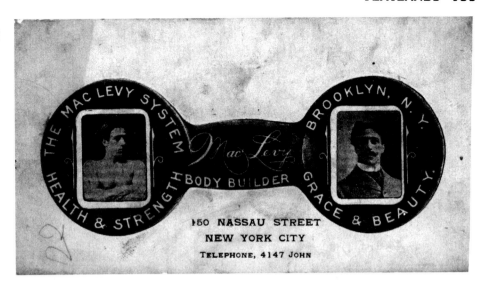

VANDERVEER PARK LAND OFFICE, 1895
Flatbush Avenue and East 29th Street

Henry Meyer was president of the Germania Real Estate Company and built up many parts of Brooklyn. One of his earliest developments was Vanderveer Park, located on the border of the towns of Flatbush and Flatlands.

This remarkable photograph, looking north, shows Flatbush Avenue in the foreground and East 29th Street at the left. The road going from left to right is today's Glenwood Road and the road which is partially obscured by the flags is Nostrand Avenue. This is just north of "The Junction."

CENTRAL HOUSE, 1922
Flatbush Avenue and Kings Highway

The Central House was built in 1885 and was located on the
southwest corner of Flatbush Avenue and Kings Highway.

AMERSFORT HOTEL, 1922
Kings Highway and Flatbush Avenue

The Amersfort Hotel, built in 1798 and was located on the northwest
corner of Flatbush Avenue and Kings Highway. It was razed when
Kings Highway was widened, around 1923.

THE JUNCTION - AERIAL VIEW, ca. 1930
Flatbush and Nostrand Avenues

Before Brooklyn College was built, the site of the campus was used for circus performances. A gridlock was created along Bedford Avenue (top of photo) with autos trying to gain access to the "big top."
The Long Island Railroad tracks are visible at the left.

STREET SCENE, 1923
Kings Highway and Utica Avenue

This photograph was taken prior to the widening of the road. The old
Kouwenhoven Homestead appears on the left. The road was known as
Kouwenhoven Place at this time. This view is from Kings Highway,
looking toward Utica Avenue.

STOOTHOFF HOUSE, 1922
1765 Flatbush Avenue

This view is looking south from Avenue J.

JAMES J. BUTLER REAL ESTATE OFFICE, ca. 1925
2131 Flatbush Avenue

John Butler was a developer in Flatlands. His son, James J. Butler, continued the family tradition. The Butler Real Estate Office is located near the corner of East 45th Street. Note the price of a home in this section during the 1920s.

LAKE FAMILY HOUSE, 1923

This building was located at 221 Avenue V, between Van Sicklen Street and West 5th Street.

STREET SCENE, 1923
Neck Road and Gravesend Avenue

Gravesend was established as an English-speaking colony chartered by the Dutch in 1645. The leader of the settlement was Lady Deborah Moody.
This view is of the north side of Gravesend Neck Road, looking west toward Gravesend (today's McDonald) Avenue.

DONNELLY HOUSE, 1923
2064 West 6th Street

The Donnelly House (at left) was built in 1873. It was moved in order to clear the site for P.S. 95. The Donnelly House was purchased by the Bergens in 1915 and relocated between Avenues T and U.

EIGHT YEARS' GROWTH IN A HARMON DEVELOPMENT

GRAVESEND RACETRACK, 1922-1930
East 4th Street, looking south from Kings Highway

When the Harmon Company purchased the Gravesend Race Track property, it quickly transformed the large tract into an attractive residential section. This promotional hand-out illustrates their achievement. Today the neighborhood between Ocean Parkway and McDonald Avenue, south of Kings Highway, is home to many Italian-American and Sephardic (Syrian) Jews. There are many Spanish-style homes in the area.

These views are taken eight years apart in the Kings Club Section of Brooklyn, which the Harmon Company opened to the public in 1922. The photograph at the top shows East 4th Street, looking South, as it appeared in that year. The lower photograph shows the same corner as it appears in 1930, well illustrating the growth which comes to Harmon properties. Harmon investors know that land is the basis of all wealth.

KIDS AT PLAY, 1924

View of Neck Road, looking east from East 15th Street.

STREET SCENE, ca. 1910

Kings Highway, looking east toward West 10th Street from West 11th Street.

STEPHEN M. RANDALL,
ARCHITECT,
BUILDER
AND CONTRACTOR.

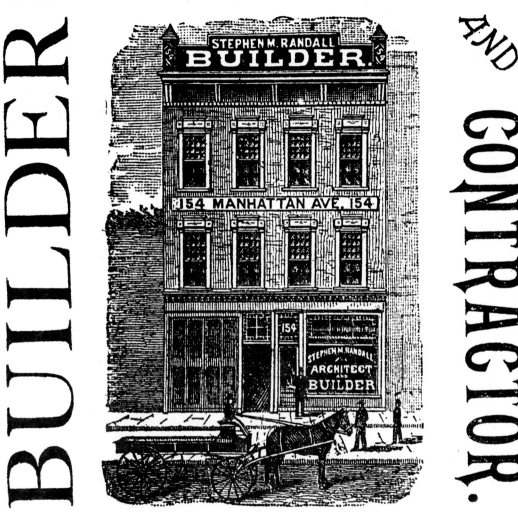

STEPHEN M. RANDALL,
Builder, Architect and Contractor,
Office, 154 Manhattan Avenue,   Telephone 179 Greenpoint.

I am prepared to build any kind of building in City or Country. Have every facility to do the largest kind of Building, and workmen for the finest Residences, trimmed in either Hard or Soft Wood. All work done in a first-class manner and as cheap as any one can do the same class of work.

Estimates cheerfully furnished. If you intend to build and have no plans will make the same with specifications and superintend the work for a reasonable price.

SYNAGOGUE, ca. 1920
955 Manhattan Avenue

This synagogue was located between India and Java Streets.

RUSSIAN ORTHODOX CATHEDRAL OF THE TRANSFIGURATION
228 North 12th Street

This landmark church was designed by Louis Allmendinger in 1922.

ADVERTISING BLOTTER, 1908

Thomas Anderson's Emporium in Greenpoint gave out this attractive blotter as a promotional drive to increase sales.

PHILIP W. BURGEY'S
Eckford Segar Store
IMPORTED AND DOMESTIC SEGARS.

No. 53 Greenpoint Avenue,

Bet. Franklin & West Sts.,   GREENPOINT, L. I.

Fine Segars, Tobacco, Smokers' Articles, Etc.

ALL SEGARS MADE ON THE PREMISES.

TRADE CARD, ca. 1880

ESTABLISHED 1855.

The Gutta Percha & Rubber Mfg Co.

MANUFACTURE

Mechanical Rubber Goods of every kind, Belting, Packing, Hose &c.&c.

Branches:
CHICAGO,
170 Lake St.
SAN FRANCISCO,
469 Market St.
BOSTON,
17 Federal St.
ST. LOUIS,
421 N.4th St.

Branches:
CINCINNATI,
141 Main St.
PITTSBURG,
102 Water St.
NEW ORLEANS,
94 Common St.
PORTLAND, ORE.
91 Front St.

A. Spadone, Prest.
H. E. Spadone, Vice Prest.
Matthew Howe, Treas.

FACTORY, BROOKLYN, N.Y.

MAIN OFFICE,
PARA BL'D'G, 35 WARREN ST.
NEW YORK.

CELLULOID TRADE CARD, ca. 1890

COUNTRY SCENE, 1900

This view of the Long Island Railroad, Manhattan Beach Branch, is
located at East 18th Street, looking north from Avenue U. Farmers
still plow their fields as the new development of *Homecrest* begins to
grow.

RAILROAD TRESTLE, 1909
Avenue R and East 15th Street

In 1909, the Brooklyn, Flatbush and Coney Island Railroad was
"raised" to an above-grade rail line. This eliminated all of the
dangerous grade-crossings. Horse-drawn wagons could now travel
safely below the trestle on Avenue R.

STREET SCENE, ca. 1910
Kings Highway from East 13th to East 15th Streets

KINGS HIGHWAY STREET SCENE, 1944
Kings Highway and East 16th Street

Before King's Plaza was constructed, Kings Highway was one of the
borough's major shopping spots. These stores were constructed from
1910 until 1930 and continue to serve the community.
The Avalon Theatre was located at the corner of East 18th Street and
is today occupied by Pathmark.

CORNER GROCERY, ca. 1915
Coney Island and Church Avenues

Gilbert Brothers' Grocery was located at 461 Coney Island Avenue, at the northeast corner of Church Avenue. Delivery by horse-drawn wagon was the rule rather than the exception well into the 1930s.

KENSINGTON RAILROAD STATION, ca. 1900

The Kensington Railroad Station was located near today's Ditmas Avenue station on the F Line. It was located the east side of today's McDonald Avenue, then known as Gravesend Avenue.

PASTRE'S AUTO GARAGE, ca. 1910
18 & 20 Ocean Parkway

The introduction of the automobile into the American lifestyle changed the way Americans lived, worked and played. Auto dealerships opened up all over Brooklyn, especially along Bedford Avenue between Eastern Parkway and Atlantic Avenue.

Pastre's Auto Garage was a full service facility, and was an authorized sales agent for Rambler and National. It was located opposite the Parkway Roller Skating Rink, near Park Circle.

REAL ESTATE PROMOTION, 1912

When the town of New Utrecht was absorbed into New York City in 1898, it paved the way for new development. New Utrecht's farms were subdivided into sections known as Borough Park, Lefferts Park, Homewood, Blythebourne, Bensonhurst-by-the-Sea, Van Pelt Manor and Mapleton Park. Today, some of these sections are collectively known as Bensonhurst. The homes listed in this real estate promotion were built near Bay Parkway, from 63rd to 67th Streets.

CONEY ISLAND AVENUE TROLLEY, 1907
Coney Island Avenue and Avenue H

This view is looking south along Coney Island Avenue. The Long Island Railroad tracks cross Coney Island Avenue (on grade). The building on the left is still extant. It is located just opposite today's Young Israel of Flatbush.

STREET SCENE, 1905
Coney Island Avenue, looking north at Avenue N.

AVENUE J, 1925

This view of Avenue J is from the corner of Coney Island Avenue, looking east toward the Brighton Line.

STREET SCENE, 1940s
Coney Island Avenue and Avenue K

This view looking north on Coney Island Avenue shows the old Vogue Movie Theatre. When this photograph was taken, two foreign films (one in French, the other in Russian - with English subtitles) were featured. That structure is presently the Prospect Park Nursing Home.

BEGINNINGS OF AVENUE J, 1908
View of Avenue J, looking east from East 14th Street.

VITAGRAPH STUDIOS, ca. 1915
Locust Avenue, East 14th Street and Liberty Street

Located just north of Avenue M in what was once called "South Greenfield," the Vitagraph Studios produced hundreds of silent motion pictures. Many silent "westerns" and Civil War battle scenes were shot on location in the surrounding farm country "back lot" of Midwood. After the advent of talkies it continued to produce films under the name "Vitaphone" until 1939. A color television studio was constructed near the site by NBC in 1952. The original cinder-block Vitagraph Studios are still extant. They are owned by the Shulamith School for Girls.

VAN PELT MANOR HOUSE
18th Avenue and 81st Street

Construction on this house was begun by Aert Teunis van Pelt in the late 1600s. It was enlarged by his son, Petrus Aertsen, prior to the American Revolution. The house was located on the Old Kings Highway. It was demolished in November, 1953.

·TRIUMPHAL·ARCH·

·SOLDIERS·AND·SAILORS·MONUMENT·
·BROOKLYN·

·DIMENSIONS·
·TOTAL HEIGHT - 71·FT·0·INS·
·TOTAL WIDTH - 80·FT·0·INS·
·TOTAL DEPTH   45·FT·0·INS·
·HEIGHT OF ARCH - 48·FT·6·INS·
·WIDTH OF ARCH - 57·FT·0·INS·

·JOHN·H·DUNCAN·ARCHITECT·
·ROBERT·VAN BUREN·ENGINEER·IN·CHARGE·

SOLDIERS' & SAILORS' MEMORIAL ARCH
Grand Army Plaza

This Neo-Roman monument commemorates the Union forces in the
Civil War. This rendering was part of the original set of drawings
submitted by John H. Duncan in 1892. He was also the architect of
Grant's Tomb. Frederick Law Olmsted and Calvert Vaux designed
Brooklyn's Prospect Park, Eastern Parkway and Ocean Parkway, and
the City of Brooklyn (today's Fort Greene) Park.

AIR CRASH IN BROOKLYN, 1960
Seventh Avenue and Sterling Place

On December 19, 1960, the wreckage of a United Airlines is removed from Seventh Avenue following a mid-air collision.

METHODIST EPISCOPAL HOSPITAL, 1902
Seventh Street and Seventh Avenue

Front page of pamphlet designed for solicitation of donations.

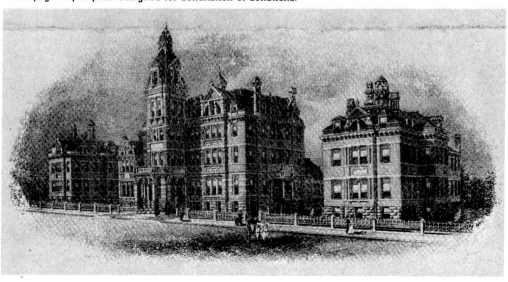

STREET SCENE, 1916
Seventh Avenue and 11th Street

THE ICE CREAM MAN, 1938

The Buffalo Bar ice cream vendor was sued by the company
Bungalow Bar for infringement.

STREET SCENE, ca. 1920
566 Eleventh Street, corner Eighth Avenue

STREET SCENE, ca. 1920
1024 Eighth Avenue, corner Eleventh Street

PARKVILLE RAILROAD STATION, May 29, 1906
Gravesend (now McDonald) and Elmwood Avenues

This view is looking south along today's McDonald Avenue. The Long Island Railroad tracks are intersecting the Gravesend (today's McDonald) Avenue tracks.

EDGAR ON BAY PARKWAY, April 14, 1919
Bay Parkway and Washington Cemetery

PARKVILLE TUNNEL, September 19, 1906
Gravesend (now McDonald) Avenue near Avenue H

In just four months, the Long Island Railroad was lowered and passed
through the Parkville Tunnel at Gravesend (today's McDonald) Avenue.
The train above is the Brooklyn Rapid Transit Gravesend (today's F)
Line. The train below is the Long Island Railroad - Bay Ridge Branch.

STREET SCENE, 1924
Underhill Avenue

This view is looking north from St. Johns Place toward Sterling Place.

STREET SCENE, 1924
Lincoln Place, looking east toward Washington Avenue

This section was developed in the late 1800s and early 1900s. It is
just north of Eastern Parkway. This photograph shows new apartment
buildings constructed after World War I. The Strand Vaudeville House
is located on the right.

STREET SCENE, 1924
Lincoln Place, looking west toward Washington Avenue

HOOK and LADDER 132, 1915
489 St. Johns Place

FREDERICK W. STUHLER'S TAVERN, 1908
Old No. 27 Forest Avenue

The Grand Annual Outing of the East Williamsburgh Chowder Club met outside Stuhler's Tavern on Labor Day for an outing to Willow Grove in Flushing. It was a politically active bunch holding brooms to signify the ousting of Queens Borough President Bermel, who was in scandel over a land deal where he had the city purchase Kissena Park, which was privately owned by his friends.
Ridgewood is partially located in Brooklyn and partially located in Queens.

THE BAY - AERIAL VIEW, ca. 1930s

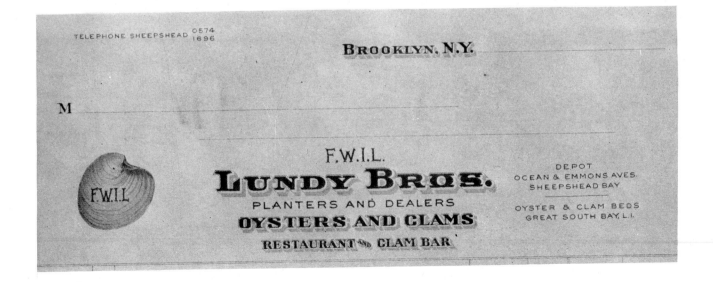

SHEEPSHEAD BAY RESTAURANT, 1934
Emmons Avenue

These old wood-frame buildings were kept warm by the heat of pot-belly stoves. The men seated in this restaurant are aware that their building would be condemned and replaced by the new bulkhead along Sheepshead Bay.

LUNDY BROS. DOCK, 1931

Lundy Brothers were most famous for their landmark restaurant. Before the bulkheads were installed by the WPA in the mid 1930s, Lundy's and other businesses were located on the Bay side of Emmons Avenue. Frederick Lundy entered politics and became alderman in one of Brooklyn's districts in 1902. The family had been in the fish business since the late 1800s.

STREET SCENE, 1905
Ocean Avenue, looking north toward Voorhies Avenue.

A 3976 Ocean Avenue, Sheepshead Bay, L. I.

Dear Florence! — Lulu and I are now at the Bay getting the air for good of our health. How are you enjoying yourself? I suppose you are having one fine time. Write me a little some time
May.

SHEEPSHEAD BAY CLUB, 1905
Ocean Avenue

Sheepshead Bay was an elegant playground for the rich and famous.

RAILROAD CROSSING, 1903
Sheepshead Bay Road and East 16th Street

The Long Island Railroad, Manhattan Beach Branch, ran at grade on Sheepshead Bay Road in 1903. The building in the center is still extant and occupied by the Champagne Auto Parts Company. Jerome Avenue is located on the right side of the photograph.

DUTCH HOMESTEAD, 1924

The Emans House was located north of Avenue Y, between East 14th and East 15th Streets. It was built in 1857. Bessie Hill, an American of African descent, owned the house from 1912 until its demolition around 1925.

STREET SCENE, 1908

Sheepshead Bay Road, looking west toward the Brighton Beach Line. In the distance is the old St. Mark's R.C. Church. This wood-frame structure burned in 1929. Services were conducted at the Sheldon Theatre until the present church on Ocean Avenue and Avenue Z was completed.
The Central Hotel, a noted 19th century establishment, is visible on the right.

SEA VIEW GARDENS, ca. 1930

These bungalows were located near Nostrand Avenue, between
Emmons Avenue and The Bay.

LOSCHEN'S CHOCOLATE SHOPPE, ca. 1915
502 Prospect Avenue

Herman and John Loschen operated this store at the corner of Fifth Avenue for many years. The term *South Brooklyn* is not commonly used these days. It was named so because it was, until 1898, the southernmost section of the City of Brooklyn.
It refers to sections of the old Eighth and Tenth Wards, surrounded approximately by Union Street, Fifth Avenue, 39th Street and the Gowanus Bay. Some have considered parts of Red Hook and Sunset Park within the boundaries of South Brooklyn.

STREET SCENE, 1912
Hamilton Avenue

The Gowanus Expressway today shadows this entire portion of Hamilton Avenue. This view of Hamilton Avenue is looking north from Prospect Avenue toward 16th Street. The Gowanus Canal Bridge is three blocks in the distance.

WILLIAMSBURG BRIDGE UNDER CONSTRUCTION, 1903

Before the Williamsburg Bridge was constructed, ferry service linked Williamsburg with Manhattan's Lower East Side. This view of the Williamsburg Bridge is from South 6th Street, looking west from Dunham Place towards Kent Avenue.

STREET SCENE, March, 1929
401 Grand Street

STREET SCENE, October, 1928
Wythe Avenue and Grand Street

SAMUEL LIPPMANN.

JULIUS LIPPMANN.

LIPPMANN BROS.

COMMISSION MERCHANTS,

ESTABLISHED 1870.

FRUITS AND PRODUCE,

BUTTER, EGGS, POULTRY & GAME.

12 & 123 WALLABOUT MARKET.

REFERENCES

MANUFACTURERS NATIONAL BANK, BROOKLYN, N.Y.
WALLABOUT BANK, BROOKLYN, N.Y.
FIRST NATIONAL BANK, BROOKLYN, N.Y.

BROOKLYN, N.Y.

LIPPMANN BROS.

LIPPMANN BROS.

12 WASHINGTON AVE.

123 WEST AVE.

ADVERTISEMENT, 1891

ESTABLISHED OVER THIRTY YEARS.

Ph. Strauss & Co.,

Clothiers and Merchant Tailors.

245 GRAND STREET.

New Store,

Bet. 6th and 7th.   Brooklyn, E. D.

JACOB FITTING,

DEALER IN

Copper & Tin Ware, Stoves &c.,

TIN ROOFER AND SHEET IRON WORKER,

No. 285 Grand Street, Williamsburgh, L. I.

Deutscher Blecharbeiter.

BUSINESS CARD, ca. 1865

TRADE CARD, ca. 1885
ARBUCKLE COFFEE STORES
Williamsburg Waterfront

"ARIOSA" COFFEE.

839,972 POUNDS ROASTED DAILY.

THE ENORMOUS CONSUMPTION OF THIS POPULAR BRAND GIVES PROOF THAT FOR STRENGTH, PURITY AND DELICIOUSNESS IT HAS NO EQUAL.

76

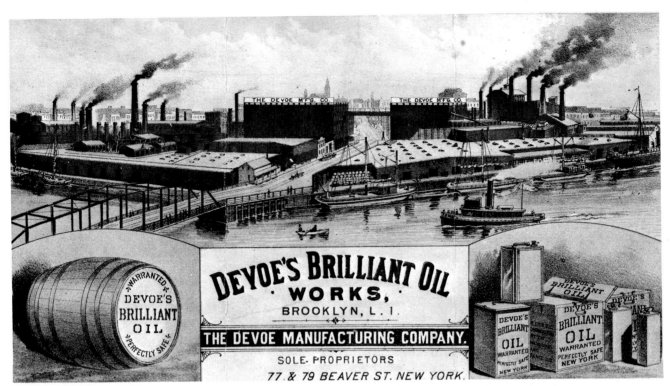

TRADE CARD, ca. 1885

MARBLE GAME, 41 Sumpter Street, 1915

Kids wearing knickers would often play marbles, skelly or shoot a game of dice on Brooklyn's legendary sidewalks.

ADVERTISEMENT, 1891

ADVERTISEMENT, 1891

HEWITT TRUCK, ca. 1915

This chain-driven vehicle with uneven size wheels was capable of carrying more cargo than horse-drawn vehicles. The advent of the truck as a mode of distribution of goods increased the production of Brooklyn's large factories. Still heavily reliant upon railroads and ships, the factories could now speed up delivery of raw materials for manufacture and bring greater quantities of products to places where railroads could not go. This truck was owned by the Mollenhauer Sugar Refinery, located at Kent and Division Avenues. Mollenhauer employed five hundred workers in 1893.

ADVERTISING BLOTTER, ca. 1920s

Along with Ebinger's and Entenmann's, the Dugan Brothers provided quality baked goods to Brooklyn's numerous households.

TELEPHONE 3693 WILLIAMSBURG

Dugan Bros.' Home Baking

Made by clean bakers in a clean, modern, sunny, airy Bakery

Fine Home-made Bread, Cakes, Pies, Crullers, Biscuits, etc.

A polite salesman with sales wagon is now serving this section of the city

BROADWAY, NEAR MARCY AVE. BROOKLYN

THIS PICTURE SHOWS THE OVEN SECTION OF OUR NEW BAKERY

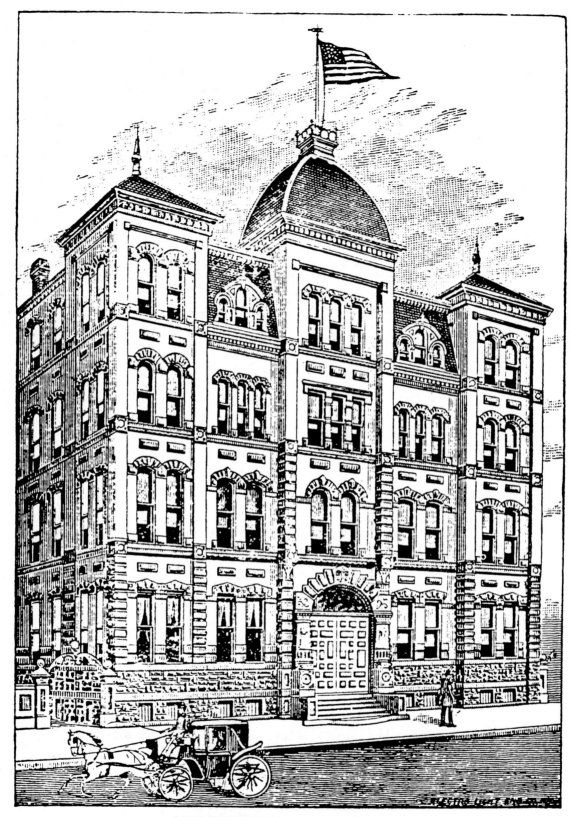

LONG ISLAND BUSINESS COLLEGE, 1904
143-149 South 8th Street, between Bedford and Driggs Avenues

The school was purchased by the City of New York for the sum of $70,000 from the estate of Henry C. Wright. The building was acquired for the use by the Continuation School to take the place of P.S. 166 on South 4th Street near Havemeyer Street, which building has been reduced in size by cutting through Grand Street Extension and had subsequently been condemned.

WILLIAM NOLL,

Wholesale Dealer in Imported & Domestic

Wines and Liquors,

No. 75=77 EWEN STREET,

Corner McKibbin St., BROOKLYN, N. Y.

Families Supplied and Prompt Attention paid to all Orders.

⁜ W E I N - S T U B E . ⁜

ADVERTISEMENT, 1891

TRADE CARD, 1881

Anti-Chinese immigrant sentiments are expressed in this Advertisement. It was common during this period.

OLDEST SYNAGOGUE IN BROOKLYN, ca. 1900
274 Keap Street

In 1850, the first Jewish congregation in Brooklyn was organized by a group of German Jews. Kahal Kodesh Beth Elohim, later called Beth Elohim, followed the Orthodox tradition at its outset. However, with the completion of its elegant temple in 1876, it adopted the Reform ritual. The Hebrew abbreviations, K'K'B'E' still appear on the building's façade. The structure was designed in High Victorian Gothic by architect William B. Ditmars.

Following the arrival of thousands of Eastern European Jews after the turn of the century, the original German Jews moved south to Bedford-Stuyvesant. In 1921, Temple Beth Elohim merged with another Reform congregation in the area, Temple Israel, which was located at Bedford and Lafayette Avenues. This merger resulted in the creation of the Union Temple. The Union Temple is located on Eastern Parkway, near Grand Army Plaza.

The Keap Street building was later used by an Orthodox congregation. In 1979, the building was sold to the Pupa Chassidim. It is now used as a girl's yeshiva.

MOORE STREET MARKET, ca. 1905

Although not as vibrant as Brownsville's Belmont Avenue or Manhattan's Essex Street, Williamsburg's Moore Street Market provided necessities for the immigrant families who resided nearby. This view is looking east on Moore Street from Graham Avenue.

LOOKING EAST o   m Ave-about 19C

GRAND OPENING CELEBRATION, 1905
19 Varet Street

Congregation Ohav Scholem was organized in 1893. Seen here is the grand opening celebrations of their new synagogue in 1905. In 1905-06, hundreds of thousands of Eastern European Jews fled the Ukraine following the brutal pogroms. Many of these people settled in the Williamsburg section of Brooklyn.

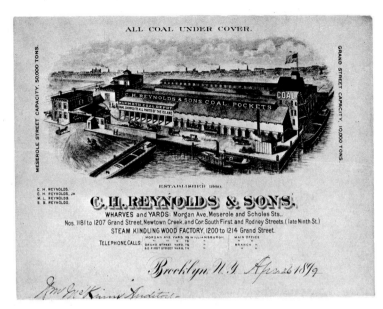

LETTERHEAD, 1899

STREET SCENE, ca. 1912
Wythe Avenue

Although considered part of Williamsburg for years, the old 19th Ward was never really part of Williamsburg. It was known as East Brooklyn. When the City of Williamsburg merged with the City of Brooklyn in 1855, Wards 13, 14, 15 and 16 were added to the City of Brooklyn. Those four wards comprised Williamsburg. The 19th Ward was bounded by the Navy Yard, Division Avenue, Broadway and Flushing Avenue. Division Avenue actually "divided" the Cities of Brooklyn and Williamsburg. The "h" in Williamsburg was dropped after the merger, but the Williamsburgh Bank still uses it. This view on Wythe Avenue is looking north from Taylor Street toward Clymer Street..

TRADE CARD, ca. 1880

BUSINESS ENVELOPE, 1932

TRADE CARD, ca. 1885

ADVERTISEMENT, 1891

STREET SCENE, 1926

Eleventh Avenue, looking north from Prospect Avenue. P.S. 154 is seen in the distance. Even further away is Prospect Park. The Prospect Expressway cut through this area in 1959.

OPENING OF THE PROSPECT EXPRESSWAY, 1959

This relatively new road connects Ocean Parkway in Flatbush to the Gowanus Expressway in South Brooklyn. It divides Windsor Terrace as it makes its way between Prospect Park and Greenwood Cemetery. Although it alleviates traffic in the area, it nearly destroyed one of Brooklyn's loveliest neighborhoods. This view is looking southeast from Seventh Avenue.

CATALOG

WELCOME BACK TO BROOKLYN
by Brian Merlis   172pp   ISBN 1-878741-14-4   **$19.95** (plus $2.50 shipping)

THE COMPLETE UNITED STATES JEWISH TRAVEL GUIDE
by Oscar Israelowitz   455pp   ISBN 1-878741-13-6   **$14.95** (plus $2.50 shipping)

SYNAGOGUES OF THE UNITED STATES
A Photographic & Architectural Survey
by Oscar Israelowitz   200pp   ISBN 1-878741-11-X   **$29.95** (plus $2.50 shipping)
              [Paperback]   ISBN 1-878741-09-8   **$24.95** (plus $2.50 shipping)

GUIDE TO JEWISH EUROPE
by Oscar Israelowitz   355pp   ISBN 1-878741-19-5   **$14.95** (plus $2.50 shipping)

ITALY JEWISH TRAVEL GUIDE
by Annie Sacerdoti   200pp   ISBN 1-878741-15-2   **$14.95** (plus $2.50 shipping)

CANADA JEWISH TRAVEL GUIDE
by Oscar Israelowitz   196pp   ISBN 1-878741-10-1   **$9.95** (plus $2.00 shipping)

THE UNITED STATES HOLOCAUST MEMORIAL MUSEUM
          & WASHINGTON, D.C. GUIDE
by Oscar Israelowitz   126pp   ISBN 1-878741-16-0   **$7.95** (plus $2.00 shipping)

NEW YORK CITY JEWISH TRAVEL GUIDE
by Oscar Israelowitz   196pp   ISBN 1-878741-17-9   **$11.95** (plus $2.00 shipping)

LOWER EAST SIDE GUIDE
by Oscar Israelowitz   126pp   ISBN 1-878741-04-7   **$6.95** (plus $2.00 shipping)

ELLIS ISLAND GUIDE
With Lower Manhattan
by Oscar Israelowitz   126pp   ISBN 1-878741-01-2   **$7.95** (plus $2.00 shipping)

EAT YOUR WAY THROUGH AMERICA & CANADA
A Kosher Dining Guide.
by Oscar Israelowitz   126pp   ISBN 1-878741-03-9   **$5.95** (plus $1.50 shipping)

GUIDE TO THE JEWISH WEST
by Oscar Israelowitz   320pp   ISBN 1-878741-06-3   **$11.95** (plus $2.00 shipping)

EARLY VIEWS OF BOROUGH PARK
by Oscar Israelowitz   96pp   ISBN 1-878741-12-8   **$4.95** (plus $1.50 shipping)

FLATBUSH GUIDE
by Oscar Israelowitz   126pp   ISBN 0-9611036-9-8   **$4.95** (plus $2.00 shipping)

CATSKILLS GUIDE
by Oscar Israelowitz   126pp   ISBN 1-878741-07-1   **$4.95** (plus $2.00 shipping)

NEW YORK CITY SUBWAY GUIDE
by Oscar Israelowitz   260pp   ISBN 0-9611036-7-1   **$6.95** (plus $2.00 shipping)

GUIDE TO JEWISH CANADA & U.S.A.
Volume I - Eastern Provinces
by Oscar Israelowitz   326pp   ISBN 0-9611036-8-X   **$11.95** (plus $2.50 shipping)

GUIDE TO JEWISH U.S.A.
Volume II - The South
by Oscar Israelowitz   176pp   ISBN 0-9611036-6-3   **$9.95** (plus $2.00 shipping)

THE BEST JEWISH TRAVEL GUIDE TO ISRAEL
by Asher Israelowitz   ISBN 1-878741-18-7   320 pages
                    $19.95 (plus $2.50 shipping)

Israelowitz Publishing

P.O.Box 228 Brooklyn, NY 11229

Tel. (718) 951-7072   FAX (718) 951-7072

INDEX